It seems like I'm always searching
for a way to tell you how
wonderful I think you are.

So I'm going to ask this book
to help me convey
a few thoughts that
I would love to share with you...

Blue Mountain Arts®
Bestselling Titles

By Susan Polis Schutz:
To My Daughter, with Love, on the Important Things in Life
To My Son, with Love
I Love You

Is It Time to Make a Change?
by Deanna Beisser

To the Love of My Life
by Donna Fargo

100 Things to Always Remember... and One Thing to Never Forget
To the One Person I Consider to Be My Soul Mate
By Douglas Pagels

A Lifetime of Love ...Poems on the Passages of Life
by Leonard Nimoy

Anthologies:
Always Believe in Yourself and Your Dreams
For You, My Daughter
I Love You, Mom
I'm Glad You Are My Sister
Marriage is a Promise of Love
May You Always Have an Angel by Your Side
Take Each Day One Step at a Time
Teaching and Learning Are Lifelong Journeys
There Is Greatness Within You, My Son
Think Positive Thoughts Every Day
To My Child
With God by Your Side ...You Never Have to Be Alone

For You, Just Because

You're
Very Special

to Me

For someone who
deserves to know
how wonderful they are

Special Updated Edition

Douglas Pagels

Blue Mountain Press™

Boulder, Colorado

Library of Congress Catalog Card Number: 91-73570
ISBN: 0-88396-347-7

Acknowledgments: This book, written by Douglas Richard Pagels, was originally published
under a pseudonym. Special thanks to Susan and Stephen and the Blue Mountain Arts®
creative staff.

Certain trademarks are used under license.

Printed in the United States of America.
Second printing of this edition: 2003

 This book is printed on recycled paper.

This book is printed on fine quality, laid embossed, 80 lb. paper. This paper has
been specially produced to be acid free (neutral pH) and contains no groundwood
or unbleached pulp. It conforms with all the requirements of the American National
Standards Institute, Inc., so as to ensure that this book will last and be enjoyed by
future generations.

Blue Mountain Arts, Inc.

P.O. Box 4549, Boulder, Colorado 80306

CONTENTS

I want this book to put
a smile on your face...

I want it to remind you
that you have been on my mind.
I want it to tell you that
    I think you're wonderful.
I want it to be a beautiful part
    of this day.

And I want it to help you remember
    — every time you see it
        in the days yet to be —
    that this book was given to you

        just because...
    you're *very special* to me.

24 Things to
Always Remember...
and One Thing to Never Forget

Your presence is a present to the world.
You're unique and one of a kind.
Your life can be what you want it to be.
Take the days just one at a time.

Count your blessings, not your troubles.
You'll make it through whatever comes along.
Within you are so many answers.
Understand, have courage, be strong.

Don't put limits on yourself.
So many dreams are waiting to be realized.
Decisions are too important to leave to chance.
Reach for your peak, your goal, your prize...

Nothing wastes more energy than worrying.
The longer one carries a problem,
    the heavier it gets.
Don't take things too seriously.
Live a life of serenity, not a life of regrets.

Remember that a little love goes a long way.
Remember that a lot... goes forever.
Remember that friendship is a wise investment.
Life's treasures are people... together.

Realize that it's never too late.
Do ordinary things in an extraordinary way.
Have health and hope and happiness.
Take the time to wish upon a star.

And don't ever forget...
    for even a day... how very special you are.

The lucky people you're close to are so blessed
with the good things you bring to their lives.
It is *such a privilege* to know someone who
brings so many smiles to the day.

Do You Know
How Important You Are
to Me?

I know you probably wonder
from time to time
    what you mean to me.
So I'd like to share this thought
    with you, to tell you that
    you mean the world to me.

Think of something you couldn't live without
    ...and multiply it by a hundred.
Think of what happiness means to you
    ...and add it to the feeling you get
        on the best days you've ever had.

Add up all your best feelings
and take away all the rest
    ...and what you're left with is
    exactly how I feel about you.

You matter more to me than you can
    imagine and much more than I'll ever
    be able to explain.

The Book You Hold
in Your Hands...

The book you hold in your hands
is a very special book.
Not just because it's from me...
    but because it says something
I want you to know today
    and that I want you
        to remember
            forever.

Within the words on these pages,
I want to say that
you are incredibly special to me...

You are so important
to my days — and so essential
     to the smile within me.
That certain space where our lives
overlap is the place that brings me
the most understanding,
     the most peace,
the nicest memories, and a joy that
     comes to my heart so constantly.

When you hold this in your hands,
I want you to think of me
     smiling softly at you,
and thanking you...
          for all that you are... to me.

Among the hundreds
of wishes
of wishes
I wish for you...

I want you to have
an understanding
of how nice it is for me

...just to have
you here.

A Thought to Remember

It would bring me more joy than I can say
if you would never forget
    — not even for a single day —
how wonderful you are...
    in my eyes and in my heart.

I'm so often at a loss to find the words
to tell you how much you mean to me.
In my imagination, I compare you with
things like the sunshine in my mornings,
the most beautiful flowers in the fields, and
the happiness I feel on the best days of all.

You're like the answer to a special prayer.
    And I think God knew
        that my world needed
            someone exactly like you.

Someone Will Always
Be Thankful for You

Someone will always be thankful for you.

Someone will always cherish
the warmth of your smile and
the happiness in your heart.
Someone wants to always be close enough
to care in every way and to treasure
each and every day spent together...

Someone will always keep you lovingly
    in mind
    and will welcome every opportunity
    to find you in happy thoughts.

Someone will always know that life
    is good because of you, and that tomorrow
    has a bright and shining hope that
    wouldn't be there if you weren't here today.
Someone will always try to find the words
    to thank you for filling life with
    dreams come true and with beautiful
    memories.

Someone will always be thankful for you.

    ...And that someone
    will always be me.

Your name
will always remain
in my heart

It will be spoken
and shared in the
gentlest of prayers...

And you will be
with me
forever.

A Little Note with a Lot of Love

Sometimes we need
reminders in our lives
of how much
people care.

If you ever get that feeling,
I want you to remember this...

Beyond words that can even begin
to tell you how much,
I hold you and your happiness
within my heart each and
every day.

I am so grateful for you, and so thankful
to the years that have given me
so much to be thankful for.

I Care So Much About You

I care about you
   more than I can say.
And that caring and that feeling
have a meaning that is more precious
to me than I can explain.

But let me try to tell you this...

Saying "I care" means that I will always
   do everything I can to understand...

It means that you can trust me.
It means that you can tell me
    what's wrong.
It means that I will try to fix what I can,
that I will listen
    when you need me to hear, and that
— even in your most difficult moment —
    all you have to do is say the word,
        and your hand and my hand
            will not be apart.

It means that whenever you speak to me,
whether words are spoken through a smile
    or through a tear...
        I will listen with all my heart.

I wouldn't trade the days
I've spent with you for anything.

Well... maybe just one thing.

A million more just like them.

You are a truly special person.

Even if you were only
half as wonderful
as you are...

You'd still be
twice as nice
as anyone I've ever known.

Our Special Prayer

These are our wishes, our dreams:
That we may always be more than
    close; that nothing will come
    between the bond we share.
That I will always be there for you,
    as you will be for me.
That we will listen with love.
That we will share truths
    and treasured memories.
That we will trust and talk things out.
That we will understand.

That wherever you go, you will be
    in my heart,
and your hand will be
    in my hand.

If I Could Write a Poem

If I could write a poem,
I'd begin by telling you
    how much I cherish
        all the beautiful things about you.

I'd tell you that feelings like
the ones I feel for you are some of the
most special gifts life has to give...
    and that in this life we live,
        you... are one in a million.

And before my
    poem was through...
I would find a way
to tell you that there may be
a lot of folks who help to
    brighten up this world...

but none of them holds a candle to you.

If someone were to ask me...

...the secrets of happiness and
gratitude and serenity, I know
exactly what I'd do.

I'd tell them to make sure
that they have a person
in their lives
who's as precious,
as special,
and as wonderful...

as you.

I find myself
    thinking about you
so much of the time...

About how lucky I am
to have you as a
    part of my days;
about what a good person you are;
about everything you do for me,
    the obvious things
        and all the little things
        that you might not even
            know that you do...
and about all the things
    you contribute to making my life
        nicer than it's ever been.

If it weren't for you,
    I wouldn't have half the happiness
    that I feel inside.
I don't know what magic it is
    that makes people
    as wonderful as you...
        but I'm sure glad that it works.

It takes a certain kind of person
to be special.

It takes someone who is
really wonderful; someone who
lights up this little corner of the world
with feelings of friendship and love
and understanding. It takes a truly
unique personality and a knack for
making life happier and more rewarding...

It takes someone who's willing to take the time.
It takes an individual who is able to
open up and share their innermost feelings
with another. It takes someone who makes
the path of life an easier and more
beautiful journey. It takes a rare
combination of many qualities,
    interwoven with another person's life.

    It takes a certain kind of person
        to be special.

    It takes someone
        ...exactly like you.

You're appreciated so much! Your kindness, the generous giving of your time, and the way you inspire a warmth that shines through in all you do... all these things combine to make *such a difference.* Day in and day out, you are one of the special people who helps to make this world a better place to be.

I Don't Know
What I'd Do Without You

To you:

For keeping my spirits up.
For never letting me down.
For being here for me.
For knowing I'm there for you.

For bringing so many smiles my way.
For being sensitive to my needs.
For knowing just what to say.
For listening better than anyone else.

For bringing me laughter.
For bringing me light.
For understanding so much about me.
For trusting me with so much about you.

For being the best.
For being so beautiful.

    I don't know what I'd do
       ...without you.

If the World Could Give Me Only One Special Person

I would want that person
to be someone I could share
a real understanding with;
someone I could be completely
open and honest with; someone
who had qualities I admired;
someone whose interests and
outlooks were interwoven with mine...

I would want that special person
to bring the gift of laughter to my heart
and to have no fear of crying on my shoulder.
I would want that person to be a reason
for me to smile through the seasons of my life.
I would want that person to be the joy
in many of my best memories, and the thankful
thought that tomorrow will always be happy, too.

If the world could give me
only one special person...

I would want that person to be you.

I wish you happiness, each and every day,
in return for all the joy you bring to life.

I can't begin to thank you for everything;
my simple words don't do you justice.

But my heart knows how I feel,
      and now... maybe you do, too.

People like you
are few and far between.
You are the special
    kind of person
        the world needs more of...

People like you
make everything so much nicer;
you have a marvelous ability
to turn happiness into joy
and sadness into understanding.

You are appreciated beyond words,
    because people like you
        mean the world to...
            people like me.

Just a Little Thought for You to Keep

Though I can't always be there
with you, these words can be.
So I want you to save this
in a special place and,
every now and then,
think of me.

I want you to set this aside and
remember it when you're feeling
wonderful,
so it can remind you that
that's exactly how you make me feel...

I want you to set this aside and
save it for the days when things
haven't necessarily gone as planned,
and the clouds are hanging around
a little longer than they should.
And maybe it will help to cheer you up.

When you get home in the days to come
    and see this book
sitting on your dresser or your shelf,
remember that I'm here,
    smiling to think
        of all the wonderful
            things about you.

It's so nice to know... that words like
these can stay beside you... and a book
like this can help to remind you, every
time you see it in all the days to come...

that no one
     is more special to me
          than you are.

Hearts and souls like ours will always be close.

We could be separated from one another by great distances and long passages of time. And yet, upon meeting again, we would simply continue on as though we'd never been apart. Others would wonder... why is that, and how can that be? And the answer is...

in truth, we will never be apart.

I am so comforted by that knowledge.

No matter what happens — I'll always have you, you'll always have me, and we'll *always* be together.

For All that You Are to Me

Having someone like you in my life is like having a wish come true.

You are a blessing and a miracle. You are a guiding light. You are a reminder that everything is all right. You and I are on the same wavelength; you always understand. You do more than hear; you listen. You smooth out the rough edges and offer a hand. You like me... for me. You let me know that — with you — I can just be myself. With you, I know that I never have to hide. I can be exactly who I am inside...

You know how I feel. You have insight into my very soul. You know the big and little things. My highs and lows. My special dreams. You know where my "Achilles' heel" is, but that secret stays between us two. You know what hurts and what helps, and you come to the rescue. When things aren't right, you throw me a rope and help me hang in there.

You and I share so much: Our shortcomings. Our highest hopes. Our serious thoughts. Our silliest jokes. You are where honesty comes from and where my wishes go when they don't want to be alone.

Being with you... is what it really means to feel at home.

Special people like you

...are always thought of with
hope and happiness and
never-ending gratitude...

by incredibly thankful
people
like me.

There are a thousand things
I would like to be for you...
but one of the most important
is just being
        the someone
            you can talk to.
There are so many things
        I would like
            to do for you...
and so many things I would like
to say and give and share.

But for today
    I just want you to know
that I promise:

I'll always be there,
    and I'll always care.

Have a Happy... Everything!

May you always know
how appreciated you are.
May you never forget what a blessing
you've become to a world that could
use more people like you.
May you reap the rewards of kindness.
May your sunshine always shine through...

May love walk by your side.
May friendship sing in your smile.
May opportunity remember to knock on your
    door and surprise you once in a while.
May your memories be ones that you
    wouldn't trade for anything.
May your hopes and dreams
    find ways of coming true.

May you never forget how dearly I wish
    a "Happy Everything"
        for you.

A Thought for You

You deserve to know
     how special you are.
You... of all people...
should have the privilege
of knowing
how much nicer
     life is with you in it.

And though those words
don't get shared as often
     as I would like them to,
I would like you to know
     — today and always —
that there aren't many
people in this world
who even begin to compare
     with you.

Counting My Blessings

You're very important to me.

You are responsible for some of
the nicest smiles inside of me...
the ones that come from
memories made, feelings felt, and the
happiness that holds it all together.

I can't even begin to count
all the times that
special thoughts of you have
brightened up the day,
        made me count my blessings,
            and helped to see me through.
There is a "thanks" I quietly say
from time to time in my heart.

        And if you could hear it,
            you would hear me saying a lasting
            "thanks"... to you.

Maybe You Can Do This
Special Favor for Me...

When we're apart,
I want you to keep me in your heart
    and in your mind.

Just quietly close your eyes once in a while
and imagine me here, smiling and thinking
    such thankful thoughts of you.

For I spend so many quiet moments
    of my own
thinking how much I miss you,
    how hard it is to be apart,
        and how wonderful it is
        that you're always with me,
            here in my heart.

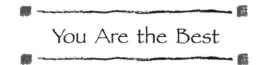

You Are the Best

Your wonderful qualities have made
a lasting impression on me that I
    will admire for as long as I live.

You give me so much to be thankful for.

You have wisdom that goes beyond
your words, a sweetness that goes
beyond your smile, and a heart
    of pure gold.

You take the time to hear my deepest
thoughts, my feelings, and my fears.

You've dried tears no one else could see,
you've helped me find happiness,
    and you've taught me that I really can
        make some of my dreams come true.

You are very important to me.
And I'll try to tell you why...

You and I share so much of what is good about life.
Things like... so many experiences
    that only you and I have known.
And so many personal feelings and emotions
    that we have shown only to each other.

With us, the ordinary times turn into great times
and simple conversations turn into honest,
    trusting talks. With us, so much is understood.
So much is everything it should be... and more.

Laughter is natural and easy. Sentiment is shared.
Hard times are softened. And the more often I think
    about you, the more wonderful I realize you are.
Whether I'm alone, or we're talking on the phone,
    or we're taking a long walk,
I know how much we both care... and I cherish
    knowing that it will always be that way.

Thank You for These Feelings

For bringing me happiness
  as though it were a gift
  I could open every day
      ...I am grateful to you.

For listening to the words
  I want to say
      ...I appreciate you.

For letting me share the most
  personal parts of your world,
  and for welcoming me with
      your eyes
          ...I am indebted to you.

For being the wonderful, kind,
  giving person you are
      ...I admire you.

For being everything you are to me,
  and for doing it so beautifully
      ...I thank you...
        with all my heart.

Thoughts for You

One of the most special
places in my heart will always be
saved for you.
You...
the one person I can always talk to;
the one person who understands.
You...
for making me laugh in the rain;
for helping me shoulder my troubles.
You...
for loving me in spite of myself,
and always putting me
back on my feet again.
You...
for giving me someone to believe in;
someone who lets me know that
there really is goodness
and kindness
and laughter and love
in the world.
You...
for being one of the best
parts of my life, and proving it
over and over again.

Everyone needs
someone like you...

Everyone needs someone who is
always there and always caring.
Everyone needs someone who is just a
touch or a card or a phone call away;
someone with whom you can share
everything that's in your heart
    or simply talk about the day
in the way that only the two of you can.

Everyone needs someone to encourage them;
to believe in them; to give a pat on
the back when things have gone right,
and a shoulder to cry on when they haven't.
Everyone needs someone to remind them
to keep trying and that it will all work out.

    I hope everyone has someone
        who's as wonderful as you.

From time to time,
I find myself thinking
about the way
I would like things to be
     for you...

I would like for you to be happier
than you've ever been in your life.
And I would love for everything to
start coming together for you...
your plans and hopes and dreams.

And you know what? Someday they will.
Because you're doing all the right things.
Because you deserve to reach the peaks
     you climb towards, and because you are
          a very special someone.

There will never be a day
     when I won't wish the world for you.

May you envision today as a gift
    and tomorrow as another.
May you add a meaningful page to
    the diary of each new day,
    and may you make
    "living happily ever after..."
    something that will really come true.

And may you always keep planting
    the seeds of your dreams,
        because if you keep
        believing in them,
        they're sure to blossom
        for someone who's
        as marvelous
        as you.

You're my reminder to never
lose hope and to always find
a reason to smile.

Would it surprise you to know how
many wonderful thoughts you are such
a special part of?

Well... there is one thing I hope won't
surprise you... even a little bit:

It's that you are absolutely cherished by me.
You always will be.

And I'm so glad that my world
        has a blessing
    as beautiful as you in it.

This is for you, for being someone whose soul is so inspiring. This is a "thank you" for having a heart that's so big and a mind that is so open. And a spirit that I really love.

It's a message of gratitude for an incredibly special person. You inspire me with your wonderfulness. You're the first person I think of whenever I have something to share, and you're the last person in the universe I would hurt or ever be unkind to. You are a treasure to my life, and I value you so much. You have an amazing knack for reassuring me.

You invite me to go along to the places your journeys take you... when you dream, when you wonder, and when you reminisce...

And you let me know that you're a willing
traveling companion, happy to join me in all
my journeys, too.

I love that about you. I cherish the fact that you
understand me so well and that I know you just
about as well as I could ever know anyone.

I am blessed by the thousands of smiles we have
shared, by the laughter that lingers in my heart,
and by our concerns that have found a place of
comfort in the sanctuary of our caring. I truly
don't know what I'd do... without the goodness
you give my life.

It seems like I'm always searching
for a way to tell you
how wonderful I think you are.

And I thought that maybe
this book could help me
convey a few thoughts
   that I would love to share with you...

You're my definition of a special person.

I think you're fantastic. And
exceptional and unique and endearing.
To me, you're someone
who is very necessary to my well-being.
In so many ways, you fill my life
with happiness and the sweet feelings
of being so grateful and appreciative
    that you're here.

I could go on and on...
    but you get the picture.

I think you're a masterpiece.

About the Author

Douglas Pagels has been a favorite Blue Mountain Arts® writer for many years. His philosophical sayings and sentiments on friendship and love have been translated into seven languages and shared with millions of people worldwide in notecards, calendars, and his previous books. He lives in the mountains of Colorado with his wife and two sons.